Nurse Log

Nurse Log

Poems by

John Fritzell

© 2025 John Fritzell. All rights reserved.
This material may not be reproduced in any form, published,
reprinted, recorded, performed, broadcast,
rewritten or redistributed without
the explicit permission of John Fritzell.
All such actions are strictly prohibited by law.

Cover design by Shay Culligan
Cover image by Mark Arron Smith on Pexels
Nurse log photo by John Fritzell
Author photo by Dawn Fritzell

ISBN: 978-1-63980-782-6

Kelsay Books
502 South 1040 East, A-119
American Fork, Utah 84003
Kelsaybooks.com

For Dawn, Rachel, and Ken

Acknowledgments

I am grateful to the editors of the following publications for first publishing my poems (some in slightly different forms) as noted:

Autumn Sky Poetry Daily: "Spring"
Bramble: "Nurse Log," "Six Ways to Summer Mindfulness"
Cottonwood Magazine 58: "Watching the Weather Channel"
Gray's Sporting Journal: "317 South Main"
Landward Poetry Project: "Playing RACK-O at the Cabin"
One Sentence Poems: "River," "On Yom Kippur"
Tiny Seed Literary Journal: "In the Voice of a Cormorant," "Wild Proposition," "Nurse Log"
Wisconsin Fellowship of Poets, Poet's Calendar: "Blizzard Warning," "Przewodow," "Swale"

Contents

Nurse Log	13
Spring	14
Uncle Mike	15
Desire	17
Distancing	18
On Passover	19
Six Ways to Summer Mindfulness	20
Playing RACK-O at the Cabin	21
Watching the Weather Channel	22
In the Voice of a Cormorant	23
Personal Space	24
Swale	25
Marks	26
The Last Boom from the Neighbor's Bird Cannon	28
317 South Main	29
Letting the Dogs Out	31
On Yom Kippur	33
Hunting for Your Grandfather	34
Wild Proposition	36
Opening Day, Oma Township, Iron County, WI	37
Przewodow	39
The Leaf	40
River	41
THE Dark-Eyed Juncos	42
Survivor	43
Blizzard Warning	44
Plucking the Red Phase Grouse	45
Today's Cold Snap	46
Warm Morning	47

Notes

Nurse Log

Nurse Log

The cedar stump that held
his cocktails,
and laid away his endless stories
of errant shots and old spaniels,
he—my father, the professor—would be glad
to know has become a nurse log,
its saw-shorn archival rings
of cleavage

bog-like to the roots of seedlings,
to a winding-sheet of thriving lichens,
to a trembling colonnade of sporophytes
on soft green lips of mosses,
and to the spring grouse
who, like me, with a breath to the eternal
vacuum and a momentary boom
now drums upon it.

Spring

The wind today
makes a quick-change
in the theater
of my winter-worn yard,

you can hear her rushing
backstage
uncovering the smell
of nightcrawlers,

high-throated cries
of blackbirds,
and the whine of far-off
eighteen-wheelers

hell-bent on speeding
things along.
And now she quickly
strips-off

the last act's collection:
an empty can of Red Bull,
a white plastic bag,
a lost hydrangea's head,

and that cold piece of Tyvek,
fallen from her shoulders,
now loosely swaddling
the trunks of the lilacs.

Uncle Mike

Whenever I think of you
at this new time of year
I think of Layman's Creek,
and how its surging trickle runs clear
over pebble and boulder,
and how the wind directs
its springtime song
even to my distant stand.
It's not much of a trout stream,
its shallow shallows
warm enough for shiners,
its narrow width
a weak puzzlement
to another season's
blood trail;
yet knowing this, in earliest spring,
you don a pair of not-so-leaky hippers,
cross the pot-marked gravel
road to the deer trail and duck
the alders to fish its small and hidden pools.
And on a warped pew of cedar,
you sit awhile, strip some line
and feed a colorful streamer
under the large ottoman of root,
far-out into the deepest pool,
where long it holds and awaits
the fervent flash,
the leanness of the native Brookie,

the twitch and tug
of your steady hand,
never minding that by then,
your head has come to rest
on the rolled parchments
of the yellow birch
and your mind, like mine,
is with the nuthatch
tapping out its tiny song
so faint in time and space
but an everlasting echo
to all those who've heard it
beside this surging stream.

Desire

Springtime tamaracks
aren't much to look at,

yet for their golden phases
late in the gray of the year,

bare limbs needle themselves,
anxious goosebumps appear,

and every spring peeper blushes
ear to ear.

Distancing

On this gray March morning, I'm traveling three hours to pick up the deer meat from last fall's harvest and noticing the tangent curves of grackles looping their way across my path, and how the swans set their pinions and ride the zephyr of the changing season, and wondering whether I'll ever make it to the butcher because of stopping, now twice, to write this all down and, then again, moving on, noticing the infinite iambs of telephone wires and the stresses of poles, where the raven sits, turning its head, as if to say, *nevermore, nevermore, nevermore,* and the guy from Texas driving like someone from L.A., too fast to notice the skeins of geese far off, moving somewhere farther off, and now I'm thinking of the crickets slumbering beneath the dead and mottled browns of Waupaca's roadside hills, as Weyauwega's red-winged blackbirds pick the ditch grit beneath the occasional sign for County K—but not to be outdone, here's a mark of punctuation, something concrete, the elephant of Highway 10, taxidermy, Wisconsin pachyderm . . . *as long as an elephant's* . . . I'm coming to the end of my tale, the end of the long, continuous strip of third grade cursive writing paper, and I've stayed mostly to the right of the dot dot dot line which separates the upper from the lower case, lower cases being mine to snuggle with, alone, hiding from the turkey vultures soaring overhead, their eyes fixed on the flooded Rat River and the deer meat in the back of my truck. It's an early afternoon in March; warmer now, and as I open the window, I hear the ancient guttural bugling of cranes coming from beyond the next rise.

On Passover

The finches are back,
nesting in the front door wreath,
counting their blessings.

Six Ways to Summer Mindfulness

Build yourself a pink tar-shingled shack
a wet-side complex
low-set in a sphagnum bog
maternity ward of snapping turtles

Trundle down to a warped dock
hiding in the August purple
of pickerel weed—look up,
imagine drawing the changing faces
of animals in the elephant clouds

Stand beneath a canopy of hemlocks
and listen to a red squirrel carry-on
its mid-afternoon conversation

Sit with a book lakeside,
feel the mossy shore
and between pages watch
morphing appendages of tadpoles

Stare hard at an exoskeleton
a mindless dragonfly's nymph
soulless rigor mortis
on the new-green growth
of a dockside balsam

Watch clover give a sloe gin buzz
its puny petals messaging
the unshaven legs of the bumblebee,
whose micro-mind is stuck
skydiving in a memory

Playing RACK-O at the Cabin

It is a little bit like gambling on the proper order of things.
The cards are dealt and racked on a close summer's evening

in late June, but then the bandit raccoon momentarily steals
the attention, disrupts the participants' competitive concentration

for a chance-view of a masked stranger through a gap
in the continuum of random tamaracks, which line the shore

between your place and the prying eyes of the neighbors.
But it is a pleasant evening with grandma as the dealer,

and the only shenanigans taking place, rest with the bullfrog
who is stubbornly stuck in slot 10, his guttural voice

refusing to join the evening's perfect sequential score,
and the only wandering eyes, those of the June bug up in slot 50,

who sharpens a stubbed pencil with its teeth and beats its fingers
against the tout sheet of the window screen,

and the only shady deal being done is done by the one in slot 15,
who slithers now from beneath the couch,

crosses the bleeding slab of the cabin's floor,
finds itself glimpsed beneath the red & white vinyl-folds

of tablecloth, and elicits a better-than-winning scream
from the bare-footed nine-year-old. Snake! Snake!

Watching the Weather Channel

I would like to spend the night
snuggled-up to your cold front,
under a heavy quilt of stratus
high in the hard Rockies
somewhere west of Steamboat Springs.

You may bring the cameras,
if you are into that,
but I will just be lying here
dreaming of the big one
striking New Orleans someday.

Category 4 you will call it,
your arm sveltely sweeping the storm
through the gulf and into my bedroom,
where I will be lying stiff,
stunned at how my cigarette bow echoes
into a desirous blanket of snow.

But for now, with the thunder past,
my dreams are with the stationary front beside me,
makeup removed, eyes closed,
only the faintness of breath
keeping her face clear of the fog.

Forecast:

*Warmer with increasing clouds
and a chance for a morning shower.*

Your arms gesturing over a storm in your belly,
blocking out Cuba, filling the gulf with your billows,
indicating that someone you love lives north of me.

In the Voice of a Cormorant

Long ago he left me,
took another shape,
and still they blame
me for eating
hatchery raised perch
and relieving myself
on this sinking island
of three-legged frogs,
oil soaked waterfowl,
plastic lids and straws,
mats of blue-green algae, everywhere;
the strangely absent
insects
and spotted salamanders
displaced;
for once,
let's talk erosion
of my coastline,
my sunken sailboat's berthing;
don't blame me for the two-legged's
shadow,
I've just been hanging out here
in this graveyard of cottonwoods.

Personal Space

As a nine-year-old
there was nothing
like the bog-standing
tar-papered outhouse
set back of the pink-shingled
two-bedroom shack,
the only flush
the wood thrush
from its nest under the eaves.

It was all there,
the entire intimate effluvium,
the sharp personal ends
of tenpenny nails,
the wet, social, non-door-knocking
springer spaniel
and its publicly displayed
mud-covered tennis ball
splat-down at my feet.

Swale

The coulee runs
dry here:

the sun & sky,
the shimmer & lie

of switchgrass,
the mettle of prairie:

a sharp pair of ears
on a kit fox,

a lean weathercock
& a gearbox

run on fear.

Marks

The entries in an old duck hunter's journal
are often unfamiliar and faded,
but then there are the others:
The Beaver House Pothole,
The Boat Slough where you winged the sharp-tail
in the fog and Miss Charlie found it,
The Engen Homestead with its barn owl
and broken-down chicken-coop,
The Cemetery at Leif's Slough where,
that frigid evening, a single swan flew over
and we heard the hush of its wings,
Mose—the town that blew away,
The Blizzard Road at Wimbledon,
The Goose Hole and Holland's Pass,
Heck's Second and The Redhead Hole,
Schlenker's, Irion's and Jack Rabbit Corner,
Red Willow Pass, Sonny's and Hagen's,
The Wigeon Hole up near Lakota,
Long Lake Point north of Erik's place,
Kussler's South Shore where the bluebill bounced
and Miley dove for it,
Miller's Rock Pile—in the snow,
The Beehive Pothole where Dawn shot her first duck
and Miss Charlie broke ice for it,
The High Wire which hung the ringneck duck
west of the Whitestone,
The Island at Rott's where the teal flew,
Huso's Pass, where Buck swam 300 yards
against the wind,

The McHenry Slough, Kussler's Fog Pass,
Charlie's Pothole, Paul's Pothole, The Hills,
and finally, The Cottonwood Tree east of Milnor
where your old man is now, pulled off
in the mown hayfield, plodding down
the left-side of the grassy two-track,
tightly gripping his cane, smartly remembered,
trailing the high-tails of the dogs,
his eyes sharp for the pheasant
just now flushed, and marked,
beyond the buffaloberry, from the right-side ditch.

The Last Boom from the Neighbor's Bird Cannon

At exactly nine-o-two,
there was a tremor
from the farmer's field,
the wild geese took flight—
a furious swarm—then
a flock of mallards followed—
speculums flashing code blue—
and a pair of cardinals—
one a quickly fading red,
the other green with a crimson hue
and tired brown eyes—
lit on the bare season's
branch to warm in the morning sun
just beyond my window's screen.
And there they sat
sharing their last seed
it seemed, for a moment—
and for a long time too
the second hand
on the kitchen clock
is all I heard—
but then, when once more
they touched their beaks,
the green one turned from the sun,
as if to see again,
and with the second boom
at exactly nine-o-four,
the red one flew.

317 South Main

A gas station used to sit on this corner,
the Hildebrands, Gackles and Rotts
used to fill their tanks here
buy some grease and maybe some chew,
if the harvest allowed it; but large scale
economies pulled the tanks on those days
and left a 650-square-foot duck hunter's house.

Now, my brother and I come in late October,
to walk the Coteau's leeward slopes
and find the hidden sloughs,
the perfect cover along edges,
enough to hide our dogs
and shield us from the certainties
of mallard eyes and wind.

The house, baked by the sun
and scaled by the knife of winter winds,
some would say, has seen better days,
but the solid wooden porch
built by my dad and cousin remains,
its welcome mat etched deep
by the hatchet blows of harvest time.

The long defunct chimney capped
by Clarence the good neighbor
mostly keeps the rain and critters out;
the door and windows have all been replaced,
but somehow the flies still manage the inside
when we're not there, like tiny government drones
they buzz around taking top secret photographs:

the waders hung upside down,
the stacked bunk beds,
the Singer Electromode wall heaters,
the covered wagon salt and pepper shakers,
long forgotten curios, the wall mirror
which makes the place look larger,
and the timeline of pictures hung

in honor of dogs and people,
the Chesapeakes, the spaniels, the labs and setters,
even Luna the Griffon in her regal pose,
standing there, watching her master, my brother
wading in deep,
setting out the decoys
and taking a measure of place and wind.

Letting the Dogs Out

On the back porch at the cabin
my ailing father and I cradle
two Ziploc plastic bags
pulled from their paw-printed tins
we sit and discuss what should be done
we consider the months and years
since the trips to the vet
we consider his cancer
we consider my scooter and walker
we consider the coming of snows,
and then we rise
and walk under the high canopy of hemlocks
across the disturbed soil down to the dock
where we sit and talk some more.
There is tension in the flanks
of our Ziploc bags, there is
anticipation and trembling.
We consider those who have come and gone,
we consider the few floating birch leaves
we consider the riffles
amidst the running gusts of wind;
even with our weak noses,
we consider the November bog
the tamaracks' golden blanket,
the droppings of deer in the sphagnum moss
we consider the red maple
toppled in the pickerelweed
we consider the impatient scolding
of the two red squirrels just above

we consider the whole outside
and the inside,
and with our business done
we open the bags of ashes
and with a shake and a flurry
and a running tsunami of dust
we release them into the lake.

On Yom Kippur

taking confession
through a curtain of cattails,
the wren winks at me.

Hunting for Your Grandfather

I would start in one of the obvious places,
the woodpile out back of the cabin,
the one with all the moss,
where the chipmunk just now
has left his neat little pile of bract scales,
remnants of a well-spent cocktail hour,
or Dad's Deer Stand Trail,
where you might, with the aid of a metal
detector, find a rusted nail or two
from his wooden tree stand,
which long ago attracted the rutting buck,
as he dragged it through the alders
in the darkness of pre-dawn, branched right
beyond the beaver pond to the south spur,
where he stopped, leaned the stand
against an aspen, and knocked his arrow.

All the obvious haunts because, as he
would say, nothing beats the opening-day
convenience of finding a full-limit pod
of grouse just a hundred obvious-yards
from gravel and also having a brace
of mallards jump
(I-never-would-have-dreamt-it)
from a hole in open-maple
just to tumble into your already heavy
game bag. Home by 10:30.

But if you are really game for it,
you can also hunt the thickets:
the Question Mark Cover, the Hump Trail,
the often-flooded Jousting Trail,
the Crazy Setter Cover and, thickest of all,
the Beaver Dam Trail. Of course,
you will not see him here,
but your dog will have a ball
and you might hear the shit-in-your-pants
startling flush of him
flying into his final sanctuary—
the black spruce—
and that will be, obviously, enough.

Wild Proposition

With this October snow,
the robin on the post
outside my window
glances at my
evening cocktail.
Not impressed,
she eyes the pale
worm at the bottom
of the bottle,
she fluffs up her
chest, considers
my line: neatly
chilled, she's out
of my league clearly,
this I know,
she twitches her tail,
twinkles her eye:
good worms
aren't found
in good bottles,
and off she flies
through the early
indifferent sleet.

Opening Day, Oma Township, Iron County, WI

Enormous flakes of snow begin to fall,
hushing our steps on the south trail.
A silent, low carpet-bombing of snow:
not even the migrating tundra swans
can see us now.

Me in my brittle lawn chair, stuck
deep in the frozen moss.
Pete pussy-footing off,
the way he always has.
Mike, well-schooled in cold places,
far-east of the old bus landing.
Layman's Creek pulsing to the Montreal.

Snow everywhere. On our eyelashes.
On our coats and caps. Whorls of snow.
Quiet snow. Slow snow.
Large, cold-silken winding-sheets of snow
covering our gun barrels,
burying us in *our own* aging
high-country.

Then a halt.

A knob in the topography
blurs the sights
of the snow clouds' bombardiers.

A shot, followed
by another.
A balsam bough smiles,
swings higher in the echo
of a fallen mass.

A whiskey-jack makes an inquiry,
asks for some lunch. Layman's Creek pulses.

Przewodow

After the November explosion,
a photograph, a marginal
capturing:

a flushed by-standing
flock of pigeons,

a peppering
of shell fragments

above the circular
steel caps
of grain bins,

soggy clusters of mistletoe
in the borderless
gray-area of branches,

a crater of hearts below.

The Leaf

It's a long way down from here
it's a long way down to the ground,
as I hang now in my brittle state
weathered and colored of age.
My blade—in a calm
curled repose—waits for winter.
My midrib—stiffened, sucked dry
by the sun's lowered slant—
no longer bears watching.

But this is not a poem about chronic conditions
nor a winding-sheet's frayed ends,
but a brighter temporary vision:
of the sensational seasonal flurry
the breathless exhibition of light
and the leap I'm about to make
into October's mid-morning sun
and how the aimless drift of my shadow
will end up swaddling your sidewalk.

River

He can barely stand
anymore,
the walker
floats him a hand—
not much—
two pair
of stilts,
skis and wheels
slow-rolled
over shag,
a late
move
played for a rush.

THE Dark-Eyed Juncos

Sometimes we call them winter birds,
little birds which remind us of cold
far-off places. They come first in fall
as the birches are reaching their
yellow phases. They don their stark
helmets and uniforms, and gather
in competition with the white-outs
of roadside buntings. I see them now
teeming on my gravel driveway,
executing the perfect Landry Shift,
confusing the hell out of the hemlock
seeds—scoring one for the little guys.

Survivor

A lone
green-winged
teal
appears
six-feet
above
soybean
stubble,
and in its
turbulent
vector
and with a
wink
of its brown
eye
blows by
that 12-gauge
virus
hidden
in the cattails.

Blizzard Warning

Wind-strummed
shepherd's hook,
behold

the kit-held
chickadee
seeking,

almost
tumbling
head-bowed,

barely
holding
the trembling,

the provisional
seed of canary
caught

breathless
just short
of the barn

in a shaft
of prairie
white.

Plucking the Red Phase Grouse

He starts with the bird in the palm of his hand
with the unction to get to it, clean it up while he still can,
before dark deepens and the edge-to-edge clarity
of sixteen degrees freezes his fingers,
but a deep need for one last look intercedes
and he holds the russet head and pulls back an eye lid,
and in the frosted mirror,
on a log bench above the garden, he sits on the rough edge
and admires, in the coldest dusk,
how the frost falls on the wild strawberries
like an embroidered swaddling cloth;
he teases the royal crest a time or two,
takes a wink at reflection,
a waxing cradle of moon's eye, dog stars;
he thinks it is not always easy to age
and sex the king of game birds, yet it is an old he;
he who has flushed now into the black spruce,
safe with the stark
decelerations, the late-rising flurry of aspen leaves,
safe with the gentle plucking-off of years.

Today's Cold Snap

Today's cold snap
put a mouse in my voice,
made the snow squeak,
cracked the maple's sap,
made my eyes weep,
and froze fast his
four
naked
little
feet.

Warm Morning

It was five below
when we hit the two-track
late on Christmas night:
the old Nissan ploughed
through the crusted-bank
downslope into the bog.
Crystalline snow puffed and
baffled away from our tired treads
then steamed off the hood
as we came to a scrunching halt in the yard.
Dad kept it running, for the lights,
kicked the snow away from the screen door,
fiddled with the keys.
We grabbed the duffels
and made deep tracks
past the snow-crowned
hand-pump, and bundle-
busted our way into the cold cabin,
knocked snow from our Sorels
and stood, knelt, and huddled
around and in front of—
the glowing face—
the flame of the Warm Morning Locke Stove.
My brother told the story
of tracking and killing a wounded
deer with his knife and hands that morning,
a hard time he had of it.

I don't remember much beyond
this, just that later, after midnight,
I went snowshoeing, swished lightly
through the still-season's powder,
out onto the frozen lake,
turned west in the northern darkness
and looked back at the place,
with all its frozen ruts,
and at the sky with all its stars and nebulae.

Notes

Oma—A Finnish word meaning "our own."

Przewodow—A small village in southeastern Poland near the Ukrainian border; on November 15, 2022, an errant missile killed two agricultural workers here.

River—In terms of a hand in the card game Poker, the River is the last of the community cards dealt and is often the card which determines the ultimate outcome.

About the Author

John Fritzell lives in Appleton, WI. A graduate of Grinnell College and employed in the financial services industry, he has had his poems published in *Autumn Sky Poetry DAILY, Plainsongs, Bramble, Cottonwood Magazine,* and *Gray's Sporting Journal,* among other places. John's debut chapbook *Thuribles* (Kelsay Books, May, 2021) was awarded first place in the 2022 Wisconsin Fellowship of Poets' annual chapbook contest.

www.ingramcontent.com/pod-product-compliance
Lightning Source LLC
Chambersburg PA
CBHW020051200426
43193CB00053B/528